Scriptural Prayer Journal

Msgr. David E. Rosage
and
Sister Marietta, HPB

Servant Books
Ann Arbor, Michigan

Published by Servant Books
P.O. Box 8617
Ann Arbor, Michigan 48107

Printed in the United States of America
ISBN 0-89283-341-6

87 88 89 90 91 10 9 8 7 6 5 4 3 2 1

Contents

Introduction

IN THIS AGE of the Holy Spirit, we are being led gently but persuasively into a more profound form of prayer which is based on Scripture. Praying with God's Word adds a broader dimension to our prayer and also enriches our relationship with the Lord. For many of us this may be a rather new concept of prayer. We enter into this method of prayer with a "listening" heart—listening to what God is saying to us personally and individually. Our prayer posture is one of asking the Lord, "What are you saying to me here and now?"

In silence, solitude, and aloneness with God's Word, we permit his Word to penetrate our mind, heart, and whole being. We let his Word find a home in our heart. We approach the Bible with an attitude of attentive listening, realizing that God is present in his Word and coming to rest in his presence with a listening mood. Sacred Scripture is not an end in itself but a means of bringing us into an experiential awareness of the presence of God. Listening quietly and receptively leads us into a more personal relationship with the Father, Son, and Holy Spirit.

Keeping a Journal

A spiritual journal is a powerful tool for recording and enhancing the experiences derived from praying with Scripture. It is an account of your journey in faith, a brief record of your daily experiences in prayer. It consists in jotting down a word, a phrase, or at most a few sentences which relate what you experienced during your prayer time. A journal is not a diary in which you record all the events of a day. It is rather a recording of the significant experiences which affected your spiritual journey in some way. It is a review, a recalling, of what happened within you while you were at prayer. Throughout the ages, masters of the spiritual life have strongly advocated the keeping of a spiritual journal. Several notable journals that most of us are familiar with are: *Confessions* of St. Augustine; *Autobiography* of St. Teresa of Avila; *Journal of a Soul* of Pope John XXIII; and *Markings* of Dag Hammerskjöld.

As we learn from history, so we also learn from our own personal experiences in life. When you recall past blessings in your life, you may be moved to a deeper sense of gratitude and your spirit is lifted. Likewise, remembering past mistakes and sins cautions you and helps you avoid a recurrence. These mistakes also show you those areas of your life where you need improvement. A spiritual journal will do the same for you in your spiritual growth and maturation.

Why a Journal?

As an aid to making progress in your personal relationship with the Lord, a spiritual journal helps you to deepen and enrich your awareness of his abiding presence, power, and love in your life. As you meet Jesus face to face in prayer, you soon discover how much your daily living is in tune with his mind and heart. Such a discovery is a basic step toward initiating a conversion and transformation within you.

A spiritual journal also makes you accountable to yourself. It enables you to be honest with yourself and assists you to see yourself more objectively. It gives you some concrete facts by which you can evaluate your present status and ascertain your progress in prayer.

Writing down your prayer experiences makes you more precise and objective. It is a mirror in which you see yourself more clearly. When you review what you have recorded of your personal prayer experiences, you become aware once again of the abiding presence of God in your life. You enjoy the loving care and concern you have felt in the past, and you find yourself responding more generously to his love. Since you become what you contemplate, this repetition enables you to be increasingly conformed to the image of Christ.

Format

The *Scriptural Prayer Journal* presents a cast of characters chosen by God to appear on the stage of salvation history—people especially called by God to fulfill a precise mission or ministry in proclaiming his Word or accomplishing his will.

We need heroes and models. An aspiring musician will carefully observe and study the techniques of a great master; a would-be golfer meticulously observes every movement of a pro; great athletes become the ideal not only of the younger generation but also of many older people; children will often copy the mannerisms of their parents. We admire and respect the men and women who have surmounted overwhelming odds to achieve great success in life. We are inspired by them and can learn much from them. The liturgy and devotional practices of the Catholic church have always directed our attention to the lifestyle of the great saints, and we are encouraged to emulate their life of service to God and to others. Therefore, one of the reasons for contemplating these passages in Scripture in which people play a vital role is to permit a transformation to take place within us. When we contemplate the humility and courage of John the Baptizer, for example, our own pride diminishes as our courage increases even though we may not be aware of the conversion and transformation taking place within us. This transformation is unrecognizable because it takes place in the heart and not in the intellect.

This prayer program offers a scriptural passage for each day of the year. The ideal procedure is to pray with only one passage each day, thus permitting the Word of the Lord to find a home in your heart. Then record what you experienced during your meditation.

There is no reason to rush through this program. Walking slowly and deliberately, prayerfully and reflectively with these Bible characters will produce a tremendous transformation in our lives. They will energize and challenge us on our journey heavenward. We will become like them in responding graciously and generously when God invites us to fulfill his will and live the way of life he has mapped out for us. I am sure that Paul would agree that many of these towering figures did reveal the Lord's glory when he advises us: "All of us, gazing on the Lord's glory with unveiled faces, are being transformed from glory to glory into his very image by the Lord who is the Spirit" (2 Cor 3:18).

Walking with these saintly people makes every step of our journey to the Father a happy, joyous experience. There is no better time to begin our journey with one of these illustrious friends of God than this very day.

Part 1

How to Pray

ONE

Prayer of the Heart

USING SCRIPTURE AS AN AVENUE to get in touch with God or one of his divine attributes is one of the most effective ways of entering into contemplative prayer. This is the prayer of the heart rather than of the head. It is a prayer of listening and loving. Our lips and mind are at rest. We simply gaze at the Lord as he reveals himself in Scripture while our hearts reach out in a wordless prayer of love.

Listening involves *being* for God and letting him *be* for us. It is basking in his presence and letting him love us. It is an experience of God which cannot be put into words. This must be what Jesus meant when he said, "Live on in my love" (Jn 15:9).

In order to enter into this kind of prayer, we must first learn to listen. The Lord wants us to come to him with a listening heart: "Come to me heedfully, / listen, that you may have life" (Is 55:3).

As we listen we are communing with the mystery of God. Listening is praying. We penetrate through our human ego with all its concerns and desires and we "hear" the Spirit of God who dwells in our hearts. We permit him to transform us by molding and shaping our thoughts and attitudes.

Listening to God in his Word is not easy. It is an art we must learn. We hear so many things around us as we live each day. We are bombarded by telephone and television, by the radio and doorbell, and a whole host of other disturbances. We have learned to turn off much of the noise and din around us. We do hear, but we seldom listen.

Listening may not be easy, but it is vital to our life of spiritual maturation and of praying with Scripture. We cannot love a person we do not know. We cannot know a person to whom we have not listened. Listening to God in his Word is a major step in knowing and loving him.

A momentary reflection will help us appreciate the unique privilege which is ours. The transcendent God of heaven and earth, the Creator and Sustainer of the whole universe, wants to communicate with us personally and privately. Nothing else in all the world should matter during the time of our prayer.

Proper Wavelength

Obviously, we must be quiet and receptive in mind and heart in order to let God's Word speak to us. At this very moment the atmosphere about us is filled with radio and television signals. We cannot hear the radio nor see the television picture unless we have the proper receiving set. Likewise, we cannot "hear" God unless we are attuned to his "wavelength."

Jesus was a perfect listener since he had no fears, no tensions, no anxieties to prevent him from giving himself totally to the Father. Jesus is our model: "He went off to a lonely place in the desert; there he was absorbed in prayer" (Mk 1:35).

On another occasion: "He went out to the mountain to pray, spending the whole night in communion with God" (Lk 6:12).

It may surprise us to discover how often the word "listen" or some synonym is used in Scripture. Here are but a few examples:

"Come to me heedfully . . ." (Is 55:3).

"Hear the word of the Lord . . ." (Is 1:10).

"Speak, Lord, for your servant is listening" (1 Sm 3:9).

"Let everyone heed what he hears!" (Mt 13:9).

"Listen to him" (Lk 9:35).

The psalmist too reminds us of the importance of listening:

"Oh that today you would hear his voice: / 'Harden not your hearts' " (Ps 95:7-8).

"Pause a while and know that I am God" (Ps 46:10, JB).

"Leave it to the Lord, and wait for him" (Ps 37:7).

"I have waited, waited for the Lord, / and he stooped toward me and heard my cry" (Ps 40:2).

The psalmist also helps us enter into an attitude of listening:

"I have stilled and quieted / my soul like a weaned child. / Like a weaned child on its mother's lap, / [so is my soul within me]" (Ps 131:2).

A Simple Method

The procedure for praying with Scripture is quite simple. Reviewing a few basic steps may be helpful for entering into this kind of prayer.

First, read the passages of Scripture for the day. It is well to do this some time in advance of your prayer hour. For example, if you are accustomed to praying in the morning, the evening before would be an ideal time to read the passage reflectively.

Second, set aside a regular time and place for prayer. This will enable you to enter into the spirit of prayer more readily. Settle into a comfortable posture which will contribute to a relaxed listening to God.

Do not plunge immediately into prayer, but take a few minutes to relax and quiet yourself. The length of time devoted to relaxing will depend upon your mood at the time. Give all your cares and concerns to the Lord and let him keep them for you while you are at prayer. Don't permit anything to interfere with your date with the Lord. You may even wish to take the phone off the hook.

Third, spend some time recalling the presence of the Lord. Remind yourself that the Lord fills you with his presence, that he loves you unconditionally, and that he is always with you: "Know that I am with you always, until the end of the world!" (Mt 28:20).

Jesus is incarnated in our world in many different ways. The

Second Vatican Council reminds us that "He (Christ) is present in his Word, since it is he himself who speaks when the Holy Scriptures are read in the Church" (Constitution on Liturgy, paragraph #7).

As you prepare to pray, discover his presence, hear him calling you by name.

Fourth, read the passage again slowly, permitting every word to find a home in your heart. Believe that the words are really the words of the Lord spoken to you here and now. Listen to what the Lord is saying to you at this time.

Find one or more resting places in the passage. Linger with the words. Savor them. Repeat them. Reflect on them in silent listening. Stay with the same passage during your whole prayer period and repeat it as often as you like.

Listen quietly at the core of your being. Soak in God's presence, feel the warmth of his love, taste his sweetness. What is he saying to you? Are you experiencing a deeper revelation of his love? A call to repentance? An answer to a longstanding question? An increase in faith for a particular situation? At the close of your meditation, make your journal entry for the day:

Date and Time: Recording the date will give you an accurate account of the Lord's work in your life for future reference. Recording the time of prayer and the length of time spent in prayer will help you to discover the most profitable time of the day for prayer and also whether or not you are giving the Lord sufficient time for him to mold and transform you.

Experience: What takes place in prayer will be personal and will vary from day to day. It may include such thoughts as:

—It was a quiet, peaceful time.

—I had an overwhelming experience of God's love for me.

—I received new and exciting insights into his Word. The Lord taught me the following things. . . .

—The Lord showed me an area for repentance. I have

promised him that I will take the following steps to change this area of my life. . . .

—Nothing seemed to happen, but I was satisfied just to give the Lord my time. It was relaxing and restful.

Personal Message

The Lord is lovingly concerned about our spiritual, physical, and psychological welfare. His presence in his Word brings us healing, hope, and reassurance. He is the light of the world, directing and "guiding our feet into the way of peace." Through his Word, God seeks to involve us in a deeper relationship with himself. When he tells us how precious we are to him, and how much he loves us, his words create a desire within us to respond in greater love to him. His words help us to establish a more personal relationship with him, which will lead us into a more complete conversion and commitment to him. Because of this, the journal entries will become valuable signposts along our spiritual journey.

TWO

Fruit of Scriptural Prayer

P RAYING WITH SCRIPTURE produces many wonderful fruits within us even though we may not be aware of what is happening to us at every stage.

Inspiration

In the first place, as we pray with God's Word, we derive much inspiration, instruction, and motivation for our daily walk with the Lord. Paul enumerates some of the values of this method of prayer. "All Scripture is inspired of God and is useful for teaching—for reproof, correction, and training in holiness so that the man of God may be fully competent and equipped for every good work" (2 Tm 3:16).

As we listen to the Lord's Word, many of our fears and doubts will be removed and most of our problems will become less serious since we will gain a spirit of discernment, insight, encouragement, and support.

Conversion

As we prayerfully listen to the Word of God, a conversion takes place within us. This will happen even though we are not consciously aware that it is taking place. It may even be painless conversion. When we expose our thinking and attitudes to his

Word, a thorough purification process takes place within us. Our rationalizations, our self-pity, our selfishness become more transparent to us so that we can recognize them for what they really are. Our self-centeredness begins to decline as we take on more of the concerns of Jesus.

A *metanoia* is underway within us by virtue of the power of his Word. How simply Jesus said: "You are clean already, thanks to the word I have spoken to you" (Jn 15:3).

The writer of Hebrews does not mince words in telling us how effective God's Word can be for us: "Indeed, God's Word is living and effective, sharper than any two-edged sword. It penetrates and divides soul and spirit, joints and marrow; it judges the reflections and thoughts of the heart. Nothing is concealed from him; all lies bare and exposed to the eyes of him to whom we must render an account" (Heb 4:12-13).

Transformation

As we feed daily at the table of the Lord's Word, a marvelous transformation takes place within us. In the conversion process we detect some of our shortcomings, our faults, foibles, and failures. By virtue of the power of his Word, we are being cleansed and purified. The transformation process is more positive in its nature. As the transforming power of his Word is at work in us, we grow and mature and become more like Jesus in mind and heart. We will develop more Christlike habit patterns. St. Paul says, "Your attitude must be that of Christ" (Phil 2:5). As God's Word penetrates our being, we will discover a great change taking place in our thinking; our attitudes will be reflected in our actions also.

Again Paul is quite insistent when he advises us to: "Acquire a fresh, spiritual way of thinking. You must put on that new man created in God's image, whose justice and holiness are born of truth" (Eph 4:23-24). He writes with the same insistence: "Do not conform yourselves to this age, but be transformed by the renewal of your mind, so that you may judge what is God's will, what is good, pleasing and perfect" (Rom 12:2). When Paul writes to the Corinthians, he returns to the same theme of being transformed by the Word of the Lord: "All of us, gazing on the Lord's glory with unveiled faces, are being transformed from glory to glory into his very image by the Lord who is the Spirit" (2 Cor 3:18).

The transformation of which Paul speaks is effected by the power of the Lord's Word. This transformation helps us put on the mind and heart of Jesus, whose image is to be reproduced in us. This is what it means to put on Christ.

There is no more powerful means of attaining this transformation than by praying regularly with God's Word as contained in the Bible.

Getting to Know the Lord

Another wonderful fruit of praying with passages from the Bible is that it is the only way we can get to know God as a personal God. It is an accepted truth that the more a person expresses himself, the more he reveals about his character, his personality, his attitudes. It is also true that the more intently we listen, the more intimately we will get to know a certain person. Similarly, the more attentively we listen to God, the more deeply we will get to know him as a gracious, kind, generous Father who loves us with an infinite love.

The formula is quite obvious. We cannot love a person we do not know. We cannot know a person to whom we have not listened. The same applies to knowing the Lord with genuine heart knowledge.

In the Scriptures God tells us much about himself. He is a gracious Father, an Abba, who loves us more than we could ever want to be loved. He loves us with a many-faceted love—a creative, caring, forgiving, healing, enduring love. These are but a few expressions of his love:

"You are precious in my eyes and glorious . . . because I love you" (Is 43:4).

"Upon the palms of my hands I have written your name" (Is 49:16).

"With age-old love I have loved you; so I have kept my mercy toward you" (Jer 31:3).

"With enduring love I take pity on you, . . . My love shall never leave you" (Is 54:8 and 10).

From the Scriptures we learn that God is a compassionate, kind, merciful Father who loves forgiveness into us. He is a God who is deeply concerned about every detail of our life. The same is true about Jesus. There is a possibility that we may be well versed in Christology yet not really know him as a Person—that we know him with head knowledge rather than with heart knowledge. We cannot know Jesus unless we have listened to him at the core of our being. Jesus tells us a great deal about himself directly in the "I am" passages: "I am the Good Shepherd," "I am the light of the world," and others.

Jesus also reveals much about himself by his attitudes toward the suffering, the sinners, the poor, and also toward his friends and foes. The only way we can know Jesus is by prayerfully listening to what he is telling us. St. Jerome says, "Ignorance of the Scriptures is ignorance of Christ." Paul was aware of this; hence, he relentlessly encourages us to walk each day with Jesus, who is the way, the truth, and the life.

Peace and Joy

Praying with Scripture daily solves many of life's problems and brings us much peace and joy. Jesus promised this when he revealed the Good News to us: "All this I tell you / that my joy may be yours / and your joy may be complete" (Jn 15:11).

In his farewell address, Jesus also promised us peace: "Peace is my farewell to you, / my peace is my gift to you" (Jn 14:27).

As the disciples were making their journey to Emmaus, they were disappointed, sad, and depressed. Jesus joined them and explained "every passage of Scripture which referred to him" (Lk 24:27). His Word touched them so deeply and so powerfully that "they said to one another, 'Were not our hearts burning inside us as he talked to us on the road and explained the Scriptures to us?'" (Lk 24:32).

Each day on our journey, Jesus will keep our hearts burning within us if we pause daily and spend some time listening to his Word.

Part II

Scripture Journal

ONE

Month One

2001
May

Acceptance of God's Plan

1 1 Sm 3:1-18
Eli submits to the Lord.

_____

_____

_____

_____

_____

_____

2 2 Sm 12:1-23
David recognizes God's plan.

_____

_____

_____

_____

_____

_____

_____

3 Mt 26:36-46
Jesus' great resolve.

_____

_____

_____

_____

_____

_____

_____

4 Acts 16:16-40
Paul and Silas accept imprisonment.

_____

_____

_____

_____

_____

Ambition Leads to Ruin

5 Gn 11:1-9
Builders of Babel.

_____

_____

_____

_____

_____

6 Nm 12:1-15
Aaron and Miriam.

_____

_____

_____

_____

_____

_____

7 Nm 16
Korah.

_____

_____

_____

_____

_____

_____

8 Jgs 9:1-6
Abimelech.

_____

_____

_____

_____

_____

9 2 Sm 15:1-12
Absalom.

_____

_____

_____

_____

_____

_____

10 Est 5:9-14; 6:4-9
Haman.

_____

_____

_____

_____

_____

Chosen People

11 Ps 51:12-19
Contrite sinner.

_____

_____

_____

_____

_____

12 Is 1:12-31
Purified faithful.

_____

_____

_____

_____

_____

_____

_____

13 Jer 24:1-10
God's people.

_____

_____

_____

_____

_____

_____

_____

14 Jer 31:3, 31-37
Least and greatest people.

_____

_____

_____

_____

_____

_____

15 Ez 18:21-31
The virtuous and the wicked.

_____

_____

_____

_____

_____

_____

16 Ez 36:16-38
Regenerated people of God.

_____

_____

_____

_____

_____

_____

17 Ez 37:1-14
Enspirited people.

_____

_____

_____

_____

_____

Communication with God

18 Gn 6:9-22
Noah.

_____

_____

_____

_____

_____

_____

19 Ex 33:7-11
Moses.

_____

_____

_____

_____

_____

_____

20 Jos 1:1-9
Joshua.

_____

_____

_____

_____

_____

21 1 Cor 3:16-17
Baptized person.

_____

_____

_____

_____

_____

Compassion of Jesus for:

22 Mt 8:1-4
The leper.

_____

_____

_____

_____

_____

23 Mt 14:13-14; 15:32
The multitude.

_____

_____

_____

_____

_____

24 Mt 20:29-34
The blind.

25 Lk 7:11-17
The widow of Naim.

26 Jn 11:32-44
Lazarus.

27 Heb 4:14-16
Compassionate high priest.

_____

_____

_____

_____

_____

Condescension of Our Transcendent God

28 Jb 38-40
To Job.

_____

_____

_____

_____

_____

_____

29 Jer 4:1-4
To a repentant people.

_____

_____

_____

_____

_____

30 Mi 6:1-9
To a wearied people.

_____

_____

_____

_____

_____

_____

31 Mal 3:7-12
To a blessed people.

_____

_____

_____

_____

_____

_____

TWO

Month Two

Confession of Sin Leads to Real Joy

1 2 Sm 24:1-17
David admits his pride.

_____

_____

_____

_____

_____

2 Is 59:1-21
The prophet proclaims the people's sorrow.

_____

_____

_____

_____

_____

Conspiracy, the Evil One's Workshop

3 Jgs 16:4-21
Delilah.

_____

_____

_____

_____

_____

_____

4 2 Sm 3:7-16
Abner.

_____

_____

_____

_____

_____

5 1 Kgs 21:8-13
Jezebel.

_____

_____

_____

_____

_____

_____

6 Mt 12:14; 21:38-41
Jesus accused.

7 Acts 18:1-17
Paul accused.

Cowardice Is a Lack of Trust in God

8 Gn 12:11-19
Abram.

9 Mt 26:55-56
The disciples.

_____

_____

_____

_____

_____

_____

10 Mt 26:69-75
Peter.

_____

_____

_____

_____

_____

11 Jn 6:16-21
The disciples.

_____

_____

_____

_____

_____

12 Jn 9:19-23
Parents of the blind man.

_____

_____

_____

_____

_____

_____

13 Jn 19:12-16
Pilate.

_____

_____

_____

_____

_____

Curiosity Seeks Satisfaction

14 Gn 3:1-7
Eve.

_____

_____

_____

_____

_____

15 Gn 32:23-31
Jacob.

_____

_____

_____

_____

_____

_____

_____

16 Lk 9:7-9; 23:5-12
Herod Antipas.

_____

_____

_____

_____

_____

_____

_____

17 Jn 21:20-23
Peter.

_____

_____

_____

_____

_____

_____

18 Acts 1:6-9
The disciples.

_____

_____

_____

_____

_____

_____

19 Acts 17:16-21
Athenians.

_____

_____

_____

_____

_____

Decisiveness

20 Gn 39:1-23
Joseph.

_____

_____

_____

_____

_____

21 Phil 1:12-26
Apostle to the Gentiles.

_____

_____

_____

_____

_____

_____

22 2 Tm 4:6-8
Paul's fidelity.

_____

_____

_____

_____

_____

Diligence Reaps a Reward

23 Ru 2:8-18
Ruth.

_____

_____

_____

_____

_____

24 2 Chr 31:2-21
Hezekiah.

_____

_____

_____

_____

_____

_____

25 Ps 119:57-64
Psalmist.

_____

_____

_____

_____

_____

_____

26 Acts 18:24-28
Apollos.

_____

_____

_____

_____

_____

27 1 Thes 2:5-10
Paul.

_____

_____

_____

_____

_____

Divine Power Unlimited

28 Ps 45
Jesus' royal dominion in prophecy.

_____

_____

_____

_____

_____

29 Col 1:15-20
Jesus, the Reconciler.

_____

_____

_____

_____

_____

30 Heb 1:1-4
Jesus, majestic in heaven.

_____

_____

_____

_____

_____

_____

31 Rv 3:7-13
Jesus wields David's key.

_____

_____

_____

_____

_____

_____

THREE

Month Three

Doubters Lack Faith

1 Gn 18:9-14
Sarah.

_____

_____

_____

_____

_____

2 Ex 14:10-16
Israelites.

_____

_____

_____

_____

_____

3 Jgs 6:11-15
Gideon.

_____

_____

_____

_____

_____

_____

4 Ps 42:2-6
Psalmist.

_____

_____

_____

_____

_____

_____

5 Jer 15:10-21
Jeremiah.

_____

_____

_____

_____

_____

6 Hb 1:2-2:4a
Habakkuk.

_____

_____

_____

_____

_____

_____

_____

7 Mt 17:14-21
Disciples.

_____

_____

_____

_____

_____

Faith Is a Firm Foundation

8 Gn 22:1-12 (Rom 4:13-22)
Abraham.

_____

_____

_____

_____

_____

9 Jos 2:1-21 (Heb 11:31)
Rahab.

_____

_____

_____

_____

_____

_____

10 1 Sm 1:1-21
Hannah.

_____

_____

_____

_____

_____

_____

11 Dn 3:13-27
Three young men.

_____

_____

_____

_____

_____

12 Mt 2:13-15
Joseph.

_____

_____

_____

_____

_____

_____

_____

13 Heb 11:8-19
Abraham.

_____

_____

_____

_____

_____

Faith Responds to a Call

14 Mt 4:18-20
Peter and Andrew.

_____

_____

_____

_____

_____

15 Mk 1:18-20
James and John.

_____

_____

_____

_____

_____

_____

16 Lk 5:1-11
Peter.

_____

_____

_____

_____

_____

_____

17 Jn 1:35-41
Andrew.

_____

_____

_____

_____

_____

18 Jn 1:43-46
Philip.

_____

_____

_____

_____

_____

_____

19 Jn 1:45-51
Nathanael.

_____

_____

_____

_____

_____

_____

20 Acts 9:1-19
Paul.

_____

_____

_____

_____

_____

The Fidelity of God

21 Lv 26:40-45
To Israel.

_____

_____

_____

_____

_____

_____

22 2 Chr 6:4-17
To David.

_____

_____

_____

_____

_____

_____

23 Ps 92
To the just.

_____

_____

_____

_____

_____

24 Is 49:8-16
To his people.

_____

_____

_____

_____

_____

_____

_____

25 Lk 1:54-73
To Zechariah.

_____

_____

_____

_____

_____

_____

26 Acts 13:32-41
To first Christians.

_____

_____

_____

_____

_____

27 1 Cor 10:9-13
To the tested.

_____

_____

_____

_____

_____

_____

Forgiveness Is Divine

28 Gn 33:1-11
Esau.

_____

_____

_____

_____

_____

_____

29 2 Sm 16:5-13; 19:16-24
David.

_____

_____

_____

_____

_____

30 Mt 6:43-48
A true Christian.

_____

_____

_____

_____

_____

_____

31 Acts 7:54-60
Stephen.

_____

_____

_____

_____

_____

_____

FOUR

Month Four

Glorifying God Is Perfect Prayer

1 Ps 57
David.
_____

_____

_____

_____

_____

_____

2 Lk 1:46-55
Jesus' Mother.
_____

_____

_____

_____

_____

_____

_____

3 Lk 5:17-26
Sick man.

_____

_____

_____

_____

_____

_____

4 Lk 17:11-19
Samaritan leper.

_____

_____

_____

_____

_____

_____

5 Acts 11:1-18
Jerusalem community.

_____

_____

_____

_____

_____

God Is Good

6 2 Chr 5:13-14
To Israel.

_____

_____

_____

_____

_____

7 Ps 107:1-9, 43
To the redeemed.

_____

_____

_____

_____

_____

8 Lam 3:22-26
To searchers.

_____

_____

_____

_____

_____

9 Na 1:2-8
To the distressed.

_____

_____

_____

_____

_____

_____

10 Mt 7:7-11
Beneficent Father.

_____

_____

_____

_____

_____

_____

11 Rom 2:1-7
Kind Abba.

_____

_____

_____

_____

_____

_____

12 Jas 1:5, 16-17
Generous God.

_____

_____

_____

_____

_____

God Is the Source of All Wisdom

13 Ps 99
Wise King.

_____

_____

_____

_____

_____

_____

14 Is 45:20-25
The Lord, the vindicator.

_____

_____

_____

_____

_____

15 Jude 5-25
Spirit of knowledge. _____

_____

_____

_____

_____

God Proves His Love

16 Wis 11:23-26
God, lover of all things. _____

_____

_____

_____

_____

_____

17 Is 43:1-7
God our Savior. _____

_____

_____

_____

_____

18 Is 54:5-10
Unchanging God.

19 Is 62:1-5
The Lord, who delights in us.

20 Jer 31:3-14
God, age-old lover.

21 Hos 11:1-11
Faithful Father.

_____

_____

_____

_____

_____

God the Creator

22 Gn 1-2
Creator of all things.

_____

_____

_____

_____

_____

23 Ps 8
Creator of man.

_____

_____

_____

_____

_____

24 Ps 139
Omniscient creator.

_____

_____

_____

_____

_____

_____

25 Is 45:11-19
Designer of the earth.

_____

_____

_____

_____

_____

26 Bar 3:24-37
Creator of the stars.

_____

_____

_____

_____

_____

27 Acts 17:24-28
Creator of life and breath.

_____

_____

_____

_____

_____

_____

28 1 Cor 8:1-6
Maker of everything.

_____

_____

_____

_____

_____

A God Who Saves

29 Is 12:1-6
God our Savior.

_____

_____

_____

_____

_____

30 Is 28:14-29
Foundation of our salvation.

_____

_____

_____

_____

_____

_____

31 Is 44:6-23
The Lord has redeemed.

_____

_____

_____

_____

_____

FIVE

Month Five

God Will Guide

1 Ex 13:17-22
Cloud and fire of God.

2 Ps 31:2-9
God, my rock of refuge.

3 Is 42:1-16
God our leader.

_____

_____

_____

_____

_____

_____

4 Is 58:8-14
Perpetual guide.

_____

_____

_____

_____

_____

_____

5 Jn 16:4b-16
Spirit-guide.

_____

_____

_____

_____

_____

Good Example Attracts Others to God

6 Mk 10:35-45
Son of Man.

_____

_____

_____

_____

_____

7 Rom 15:2-13
Christ's acceptance of us.

_____

_____

_____

_____

_____

8 Phil 3:17-21
Paul, the guide.

_____

_____

_____

_____

_____

9 Col 3:12-17
Jesus, the model.

_____

_____

_____

_____

_____

_____

10 2 Thes 3:6-10
Paul, the worker.

_____

_____

_____

_____

_____

11 2 Tm 1:9-14
Paul, the devoted teacher.

_____

_____

_____

_____

_____

12 1 Jn 2:3-6
Jesus' example.

_____

_____

_____

_____

_____

Gratitude Glorifies God

13 2 Sm 22:47-51
David.

_____

_____

_____

_____

_____

_____

14 Ps 66
A grateful person.

_____

_____

_____

_____

_____

15 Is 63:7-64:3
Prayerful prophet.

_____

_____

_____

_____

_____

_____

16 1 Cor 15:50-58
Thankful Paul.

_____

_____

_____

_____

_____

17 Eph 1:3-6
Paul praising.

_____

_____

_____

_____

18 1 Thes 5:16-18
Rejoicing Paul.

Heroes of God

19 Nm 13:25-14:24
Joshua and Caleb.

20 Jgs 4:1-9; 5:7b-13
Deborah.

21 1 Sm 17:32-51
David.

_____

_____

_____

_____

_____

_____

22 Acts 3:12-26
Peter and John.

_____

_____

_____

_____

Holy, Holy, Holy

23 Lv 11:44-45; 20:26
Holy God.

_____

_____

_____

_____

_____

24 Is 6:1-4
Lord of Hosts.

25 Mk 1:23-28
Holy One of God.

26 Lk 1:26-38
Holy Offspring.

27 Jn 7:14-24
Jesus seeking God's glory.
_____

_____
_____
_____
_____
_____

Honesty, Badge of a Good Christian

28 Gn 43:11-23
Joseph's brothers.
_____

_____
_____
_____
_____
_____

29 2 Kgs 22:3-7
Temple workmen.
_____

_____
_____
_____
_____
_____

30 Ps 24:1-6
A sinless person.

_____

_____

_____

_____

_____

_____

31 Is 33:10-16
Inhabitants of Zion.

_____

_____

_____

_____

_____

_____

SIX

Month Six

Humility, Sign of True Greatness

1 1 Chr 17:16-27
David.

_____

_____

_____

_____

_____

_____

2 Sir 3:17-28
Humble son.

_____

_____

_____

_____

_____

_____

3 Mk 1:2-8
John the Baptizer.

_____

_____

_____

_____

_____

_____

4 Lk 1:39-45
Elizabeth.

_____

_____

_____

_____

_____

5 Lk 18:9-14
Tax collector.

_____

_____

_____

_____

_____

6 Jn 3:22-30
John the witness.

_____

_____

_____

_____

_____

_____

Humility of Jesus

7 Mt 20:20-28
Son of Man.

_____

_____

_____

_____

_____

_____

8 Lk 5:28-32
Jesus eating with sinners.

_____

_____

_____

_____

_____

9 Phil 2:5-11
Jesus' attitude.

_____

_____

_____

_____

_____

_____

Humility of Jesus' Followers

10 Mk 9:33-37
Ambitious disciples.

_____

_____

_____

_____

_____

_____

11 1 Cor 15:1-11
Least of the apostles.

_____

_____

_____

_____

_____

_____

12 Eph 4:1-6
Early Christians.

_____

_____

_____

_____

_____

_____

13 Jas 1:9-11
Humble servant.

_____

_____

_____

_____

Jealousy Destroys Happiness

14 Gn 4:3-8
Cain.

_____

_____

_____

_____

_____

15 Gn 30:1-24
Rachel.

_____

_____

_____

_____

_____

_____

16 1 Sm 18:6-30
Saul.

_____

_____

_____

_____

_____

_____

17 Lk 15:25-32
Elder brother.

_____

_____

_____

_____

_____

_____

Jesus' Healing Is Divine Love in Action

18 Mk 1:29-31
Peter's mother-in-law.

_____

_____

_____

_____

_____

19 Mk 3:1-5
A man with a withered hand.

_____

_____

_____

_____

_____

20 Mk 5:25-34
Woman with hemorrhage.

_____

_____

_____

_____

_____

21 Mk 10:46-52
Bartimaeus.

_____

_____

_____

_____

_____

_____

22 Lk 11:14-20
A mute demoniac.

_____

_____

_____

_____

_____

_____

23 Lk 22:47-51
Malchus.

_____

_____

_____

_____

_____

24 Jn 5:1-15
A sick man.

_____

_____

_____

_____

_____

Jesus Is All-Knowing of:

25 Mt 9:1-8
Evil thoughts.

_____

_____

_____

_____

_____

26 Jn 2:23-25
Human nature.

_____

_____

_____

_____

_____

27 Jn 13:10-11
His betrayer's plotting.

_____

_____

_____

_____

_____

_____

_____

28 Jn 16:29-33
All things.

_____

_____

_____

_____

_____

_____

29 Acts 1:15-26
Our hearts.

_____

_____

_____

_____

_____

30 Col 2:1-3
The mystery of God.

_____

_____

_____

_____

_____

_____

31 Rv 2:18-29
Our deeds.

_____

_____

_____

_____

_____

_____

SEVEN

Month Seven

Jesus Our Divine Redeemer

1 Jer 23:1-8
Jesus, the righteous shoot.

_____

_____

_____

_____

_____

_____

2 Rom 3:21-31
Jesus, gift of God.

_____

_____

_____

_____

_____

_____

_____

3 Eph 1:7-14
Jesus, the pledge of our inheritance.

_____

_____

_____

_____

_____

_____

4 Col 1:9-14
Jesus rescued us.

_____

_____

_____

_____

_____

_____

5 Heb 2:14-18
Jesus frees us from sin.

_____

_____

_____

_____

_____

6 Rv 5:6-14
Jesus, our Paschal Lamb.

_____

_____

_____

_____

_____

Jesus Our Saving Lord

7 Is 61:1-3
Jesus' healing love prophesied.

_____

_____

_____

_____

_____

_____

8 Mt 18:10-14
Jesus, solicitous shepherd.

_____

_____

_____

_____

_____

9 Lk 2:25-35
Jesus, a sign.

_____

_____

_____

_____

_____

_____

10 Jn 3:16-21
Jesus, the Father's gift.

_____

_____

_____

_____

_____

_____

11 Acts 5:17-42
Jesus, Ruler and Savior.

_____

_____

_____

_____

12 Ti 2:11-15
Jesus offers salvation to all.

_____

_____

_____

_____

_____

Jesus, Prophesied King of Kings

13 Ps 24
King of glory.

_____

_____

_____

_____

_____

_____

14 Ps 89:20-38
King of the covenant.

_____

_____

_____

_____

_____

15 Is 9:1-6
Prince of peace.

_____

_____

_____

_____

_____

16 Dn 7:9-14
Enthroned king.

_____

_____

_____

_____

_____

Jesus, the Light of the World

17 Is 60
Jesus, radiant light.

_____

_____

_____

_____

_____

18 Mt 4:12-17
Jesus, the great light.

_____

_____

_____

_____

_____

19 Lk 2:29-32
Jesus, the revealing light.

_____

_____

_____

_____

_____

Jesus Wrought Our Salvation

20 Rom 5
Jesus, gracious reconciler.

_____

_____

_____

_____

_____

21 1 Cor 3:10-15
Jesus, our firm foundation.

_____

_____

_____

_____

_____

_____

22 1 Thes 5:1-11
Jesus, hope of salvation.

_____

_____

_____

_____

_____

_____

23 2 Tim 2:1-13
Jesus raises to life.

_____

_____

_____

_____

_____

_____

24 1 Pt 1:3-21
Jesus gives us new birth.

_____

_____

_____

_____

_____

Joy, Fruit of the Spirit

25 1 Sm 2:1-10
Hannah.

_____

_____

_____

_____

_____

26 Ps 20
King David.

_____

_____

_____

_____

27 Ps 33
A joyous people.

_____

_____

_____

_____

_____

_____

_____

28 Is 61:4-11
Joyful prophet.

_____

_____

_____

_____

_____

_____

_____

29 Hb 3:17-19
Habakkuk.

_____

_____

_____

_____

_____

30 Mt 5:3-12
The anawim.

_____

_____

_____

_____

_____

_____

31 Jn 15:11; 17:9-19
Followers of Jesus.

_____

_____

_____

_____

_____

_____

EIGHT

Month Eight

Living with the Risen Jesus

1 Mt 18:19-20
Jesus in our midst.

_____

_____

_____

_____

_____

_____

2 Mt 28:18-20
Jesus with us always.

_____

_____

_____

_____

_____

_____

3 Lk 22:14-20
Jesus' ardent desire.

_____

_____

_____

_____

_____

_____

4 Jn 3:11-21
Jesus lifted up.

_____

_____

_____

_____

_____

_____

5 Jn 6:35-51
Jesus, the Living Bread

_____

_____

_____

_____

_____

6 Eph 1:15-23
Jesus, head of the church.

_____

_____

_____

_____

_____

_____

7 Eph 4:7-16
Jesus provides for his church.

_____

_____

_____

_____

_____

Love Comforts

8 Mt 18:5-10
Jesus identifies with little ones.

_____

_____

_____

_____

_____

9 Mk 9:33-37
Jesus sets an ideal.

_____

_____

_____

_____

_____

_____

10 Lk 23:27-31
Jesus' empathy.

_____

_____

_____

_____

_____

11 Lk 24:36-49
Jesus the consoler.

_____

_____

_____

_____

_____

12 Jn 13:34-35
Jesus, the model lover.

13 Jn 14:1-4, 21
Jesus the comforter.

Love of Neighbor

14 Ps 133:1-3
Brethren.

15 Jn 13:14-15, 34-35
Follower of Jesus.

_____

_____

_____

_____

_____

_____

_____

16 Rom 12:9-21
Paul.

_____

_____

_____

_____

_____

_____

_____

17 1 Cor 13
Genuine lover.

_____

_____

_____

_____

_____

18 Eph 5:1-2
Imitators of God.

_____

_____

_____

_____

_____

_____

_____

19 1 Thes 3:1-13
Thessalonians.

_____

_____

_____

_____

_____

_____

_____

20 1 Jn 4:7-21
Beloved of God.

_____

_____

_____

_____

_____

_____

_____

Mary, Jesus' Mother and Ours

21 Mt 2:1-12
Jesus' mother.

_____

_____

_____

_____

_____

_____

22 Mt 12:46-50
Concerned mother.

_____

_____

_____

_____

_____

_____

23 Lk 2:1-51
Mother of Jesus.

_____

_____

_____

_____

_____

_____

24 Jn 2:1-11
Mary our intercessor.

25 Jn 19:25-27
Mary, Jesus' gift to us.

26 Acts 1:12-14
Mary, model of prayer.

27 Gal 4:1-6
Mary, God's chosen one.

_____

_____

_____

_____

_____

Meekness Is Not Weakness

28 Gn 13:5-12
Generous Abram.

_____

_____

_____

_____

_____

29 Ps 120
A distressed pilgrim.

_____

_____

_____

_____

_____

30 Mt 26:47-63a
Jesus, victim of treachery.

_____

_____

_____

_____

_____

_____

31 Lk 9:52-56
Jesus rejected.

_____

_____

_____

_____

_____

_____

NINE

Month Nine

Meekness Conquers

1 1 Thes 2:1-7
Sincere servant.

_____

_____

_____

_____

_____

_____

2 Heb 12:1-4
Persevering runner.

_____

_____

_____

_____

_____

_____

3 1 Pt 2:22-25
Wounded healer.

_____

_____

_____

_____

_____

_____

Mercy Proves God's Love

4 Gn 8:15-22
The Lord's merciful promise.

_____

_____

_____

_____

_____

_____

5 1 Sm 12:6-12
God's enduring mercy.

_____

_____

_____

_____

_____

6 Neh 9:17, 26-31
Merciful deliverer.

_____

_____

_____

_____

_____

_____

7 Ps 86
God is merciful and gracious.

_____

_____

_____

_____

_____

8 Ps 116:1-9
God our Savior.

_____

_____

_____

_____

_____

9 Wis 3:1-9
Compassionate God. _____

_____

_____

_____

_____

_____

Ministry, a Call to Serve

10 Ez 34:1-16
Divine Shepherd. _____

_____

_____

_____

_____

_____

11 Jn 10:1-5
Loyal Shepherd. _____

_____

_____

_____

_____

12 1 Cor 1:18-31
Chosen ones.

_____

_____

_____

_____

_____

_____

13 1 Cor 9:15-27
Paul is all things.

_____

_____

_____

_____

_____

_____

14 2 Cor 4:1-15
Fragile followers.

_____

_____

_____

_____

_____

15 1 Tm 3:1-15
Qualified ministers. _____

_____

_____

_____

_____

_____

_____

16 Jas 3:1-18
Wise Christian. _____

_____

_____

_____

_____

_____

Mourning: Blest Are the Sorrowing

17 2 Sm 1:17-27
David lamenting. _____

_____

_____

_____

_____

_____

18 2 Sm 18:19-19:5
David grieving.

_____

_____

_____

_____

_____

_____

19 Mt 5:4
Blest imitator of Christ.

_____

_____

_____

_____

_____

_____

20 Jn 11:1-44
Martha and Mary in mourning.

_____

_____

_____

_____

_____

Obedience Pleases the Beloved

21 Ps 26
David, innocent man.

_____

_____

_____

_____

_____

22 Ps 40:1-11
Happy man.

_____

_____

_____

_____

_____

23 Ps 119:25-32, 49-56, 105-112
Law-abiding citizen.

_____

_____

_____

_____

_____

24 Phil 3:7-16
Paul's faithful observance.

_____

_____

_____

_____

_____

_____

25 Heb 5:7-10
Jesus' obedience saves.

_____

_____

_____

_____

_____

_____

26 Heb 13:9-19
Submissive Christians.

_____

_____

_____

_____

_____

_____

Parents' Love, a Child's Greatest Security

27 Ex 2:1-9
Jochebed's protective love.

_____

_____

_____

_____

_____

_____

28 1 Kgs 3:16-28
A mother's sacrificial love.

_____

_____

_____

_____

_____

_____

29 Tb 10:1-7a
Tobit and Anna's anxious love.

_____

_____

_____

_____

_____

30 Tb 10:7b-14
Raguel and Edna's farewell love.

_____

_____

_____

_____

_____

_____

31 Mk 9:14-27
A father who trusted.

_____

_____

_____

_____

_____

_____

TEN

Month Ten

Passion of Jesus Prophesied

1 Gn 3:14-15
Jesus, promised Redeemer. _____

_____

_____

_____

_____

_____

2 Ps 22
The Messiah's passion and triumph. _____

_____

_____

_____

_____

_____

_____

3 Ps 69:6-22
The Messiah in prophecy.

_____

_____

_____

_____

_____

_____

4 Ps 109
Jesus, a Savior cursed and calumniated.

_____

_____

_____

_____

_____

_____

5 Is 50:1-11
Jesus, a willing servant.

_____

_____

_____

_____

_____

6 Is 52:13-15
Jesus fulfills the oracles.

_____

_____

_____

_____

_____

7 Is 53:1-12
Jesus, the Suffering Servant.

_____

_____

_____

_____

Patience, Gift of the Holy Spirit

8 Jb 1:13-22
Job's patience in adversity.

_____

_____

_____

_____

_____

9 Rom 8:18-27
Paul's patient endurance.

_____

_____

_____

_____

_____

_____

10 2 Cor 6:1-13
Fatherly Paul.

_____

_____

_____

_____

_____

11 Col 1:9-14
Paul prays for continued progress.

_____

_____

_____

_____

_____

12 Rv 2:18-29
Christians' hopeful endurance.

_____

_____

_____

_____

_____

_____

People of God

13 Lk 18:15-17
God's children.

_____

_____

_____

_____

_____

_____

_____

14 Jn 1:10-16
Empowered children.

_____

_____

_____

_____

_____

_____

15 Jn 3:1-15
Born again Christian.

_____

_____

_____

_____

_____

_____

_____

16 Rom 6:1-23
Man renewed.

_____

_____

_____

_____

_____

_____

17 Rom 8:1-17
Heirs of Christ.

_____

_____

_____

_____

_____

18 2 Cor 5:11-21
Reconciled sinner.

_____

_____

_____

_____

_____

_____

19 Eph 4:17-24
New persons.

_____

_____

_____

_____

_____

_____

20 Ti 3:1-8
Adopted children.

_____

_____

_____

_____

_____

Persecutors Followed Jesus

21 Lk 7:31-35
Christ's verdict.

_____

_____

_____

_____

_____

_____

22 Lk 13:31-33
Herod the fox.

_____

_____

_____

_____

_____

_____

23 Lk 19:45-47
Jesus risks retaliation.

_____

_____

_____

_____

_____

24 Lk 20:20-26
Jesus confounds the spies.

_____

_____

_____

_____

_____

_____

_____

25 Jn 8:31-59
Jesus faces malice.

_____

_____

_____

_____

_____

_____

26 Jn 10:19-39
Jesus rejected as the good shepherd.

_____

_____

_____

_____

_____

27 Jn 15:18-25
Jesus and the world's hatred.

_____

_____

_____

_____

_____

Persevere in God's Love

28 Jer 32:36-41
God's people persevere.

_____

_____

_____

_____

_____

29 Jn 15:1-9
Fruitful followers.

_____

_____

_____

_____

_____

30 2 Thes 2:1-17
Encouraged servants of the Lord.

_____

_____

_____

_____

_____

_____

31 Heb 6:1-20
Sharers in the Spirit.

_____

_____

_____

_____

_____

_____

ELEVEN

Month Eleven

The Power of Jesus Is Limitless

1 Is 40:9-10
Jesus' salvific power.

2 Mt 10:1-20
Apostles commissioned.

3 Jn 5:19-30
Jesus' power over death.

_____

_____

_____

_____

_____

_____

4 Jn 10:17-18
Jesus' power over life.

_____

_____

_____

_____

_____

_____

5 2 Pt 1:12-19
Jesus' sovereign majesty.

_____

_____

_____

_____

_____

6 Rv 5:11-14
The Lamb, worthy of power.

_____

_____

_____

_____

_____

Pray without Ceasing

7 Gn 18:16-33
Abraham pleads for Sodom and Gomorrah.

_____

_____

_____

_____

_____

_____

8 Ex 17:8-13
Moses prayed with uplifted arms.

_____

_____

_____

_____

_____

9 Ps 130
A sinner's supplication.

_____

_____

_____

_____

_____

_____

10 Mk 7:24-30
A mother's plea.

_____

_____

_____

_____

_____

_____

11 Lk 18:1-7
A widow's persistent petition.

_____

_____

_____

_____

_____

Prayer Is Never in Vain

12 Gn 15:1-6
Abram's prayer of faith.

_____

_____

_____

_____

_____

_____

13 Ex 2:23-3:10
The Israelites' cry is heard.

_____

_____

_____

_____

_____

_____

14 1 Kgs 18:1-40
Elijah prays for proof.

_____

_____

_____

_____

_____

_____

15 Ps 138
David's prayer of thanksgiving.

_____

_____

_____

_____

_____

_____

16 Mk 1:40-45
A leper's plea for healing.

_____

_____

_____

_____

_____

Procrastination, Our Common Fault

17 Ez 12:21-28
God does not delay.

_____

_____

_____

_____

_____

18 Mt 24:36-51
Worthless servant.

_____

_____

_____

_____

_____

_____

19 Mt 25:1-13
Five foolish virgins.

_____

_____

_____

_____

_____

_____

20 Lk 9:57-62
Unfit followers.

_____

_____

_____

_____

_____

_____

21 Lk 14:16-24
Invited guests.

_____

_____

_____

_____

_____

_____

22 1 Thes 5:1-11
Prepared followers.

_____

_____

_____

_____

_____

23 Heb 3:7-19
Israel's unheeding heart.

_____

_____

_____

_____

Providence Rises before the Sun

24 Dt 32:1-14
God supports his people.

_____

_____

_____

_____

_____

_____

25 Wis 11:21-26
God journeys with us.

_____

_____

_____

_____

_____

_____

26 Is 55:10-11
God's Word achieves its end.

_____

_____

_____

_____

_____

27 Mt 10:28-33
God's eye is on the sparrow.

_____

_____

_____

_____

_____

_____

28 1 Cor 2:6-16
God's eternal plan.

_____

_____

_____

_____

_____

29 2 Cor 9:6-15
God multiplies favors into surplus.

_____

_____

_____

_____

_____

Prudent People Motivate Us

30 Ex 18:13-23
Jethro.

_____

_____

_____

_____

_____

_____

31 1 Sm 25:2-35
Abigail.

_____

_____

_____

_____

_____

_____

TWELVE

Month Twelve

Public Opinion Has a Unique Power

1 Jn 3:1-15
Nicodemus.

_____

_____

_____

_____

_____

_____

2 Jn 12:37-43
Members of the Sanhedrin.

_____

_____

_____

_____

_____

_____

3 Jn 18:38-19:16
Pilate.

_____

_____

_____

_____

_____

_____

4 Acts 4:5-22
Leaders and elders.

_____

_____

_____

_____

_____

_____

5 Acts 12:1-24
Herod Agrippa.

_____

_____

_____

_____

_____

6 Acts 16:1-4
Apostle to the Gentiles.

_____

_____

_____

_____

_____

_____

_____

7 Acts 25:1-12
Festus.

_____

_____

_____

_____

_____

_____

_____

8 Gal 2:11-14
Peter and Barnabas.

_____

_____

_____

_____

_____

Resurrection to a New Life

9 Mt 16:1-4
Jonah, sign of Jesus.

_____

_____

_____

_____

_____

_____

10 Mt 22:23-33
God of the living.

_____

_____

_____

_____

_____

_____

11 Mt 28:1-10
Mary Magdalene and Mary.

_____

_____

_____

_____

_____

_____

12 Jn 2:13-22
Jesus prophesies his rising.

_____

_____

_____

_____

_____

_____

13 Jn 11:1-44
Lazarus raised to life.

_____

_____

_____

_____

_____

14 Jn 20:19-23
The disciples behind locked doors.

_____

_____

_____

_____

_____

15 Jn 21:15-19
The risen Jesus commissions Peter.

_____

_____

_____

_____

_____

_____

Self-Discipline Makes Us Receptive to God

16 2 Sm 24:18-25
David's sacrifice brings relief.

_____

_____

_____

_____

_____

_____

17 Mt 5:27-30
A disciple practices drastic discipline.

_____

_____

_____

_____

_____

18 Mt 13:44-46
A follower's treasure.

19 Jn 12:20-36
Jesus asks for total commitment.

20 Rom 13:11-14
A Christian puts on the Lord Jesus.

21 1 Cor 10:23-33
A disciple's disinterested service.

_____

_____

_____

_____

_____

The Single-Hearted Are Blest

22 Mt 5:8
A blest Christian.

_____

_____

_____

_____

_____

_____

23 Phil 4:4-9
A single-minded person.

_____

_____

_____

_____

_____

24 1 Tim 1:3-20
A loyal follower of Christ.

_____

_____

_____

_____

_____

_____

25 Jas 4:1-10
A humble disciple.

_____

_____

_____

_____

_____

_____

26 1 Pt 1:22-25
A loving Christian.

_____

_____

_____

_____

_____

27 1 Jn 3:1-3
Adopted children of God.

_____

_____

_____

_____

_____

Temptation Can Mature Us Spiritually

28 Mt 12:43-45
A man obsessed.

_____

_____

_____

_____

_____

29 Mt 26:31-35, 41
Presumptuous Peter.

_____

_____

_____

_____

_____

30 Jn 16:1-4
Apostles will be tested.

_____

_____

_____

_____

_____

_____

31 1 Pt 1:6-12; 4:12
Christian trials proclaimed by prophets.

_____

_____

_____

_____

_____

_____

Other Books of Interest from Servant Publications